Book B

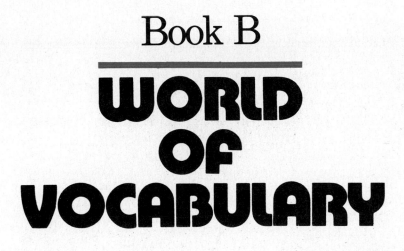

WORLD OF VOCABULARY

Sidney J. Rauch ● Alfred B. Weinstein

Assisted by Muriel Harris

Globe Book Company, Inc.
New York/Cleveland/Toronto

Published simultaneously in Canada by Globe/Modern Curriculum Press

ISBN: 0-87065-931-6

Editor: Patricia Walsh

Studio: Craven Design Studios, Inc.
Art Direction: Sandra Bence
Photo Research: Roberta Guerette, Omni-Photo Communications, Inc.
Studio Editor: Roger Gaess

Photo Credits

UNIT 1: Fig. 1-A, Wide World Photos; fig. 1-B © Jack Parsons/Omni-Photo Communications, Inc.; fig. 1-C, Wide World Photos; UNIT 2: Fig. 2-A, © Martha Swope; fig. 2-B, © Martha Swope; fig. 2-C, © Martha Swope; UNIT 3: fig. 3-A, Wide World Photos; fig. 3-B, © R.W. Young/D.P.I.; fig. 3-C, Wide World Photos; UNIT 4: fig. 4-A, © Stephen Green-Armytage; fig. 4-B, Wide World Photos; fig. 4-C, © Stephen Green-Armytage; UNIT 5: fig. 5-A, Wide World Photos; fig. 5-B, © John V. Dunnigan/D.P.I.; fig. 5-C, Wide World Photos; UNIT 6: fig. 6-A, Wide World Photos; fig. 6-B, Wide World Photos; fig. 6-C, Wide World Photos; UNIT 7: fig. 7-A, © Karen Halverson/ Omni-Photo Communications, Inc.; fig. 7-B, © Howard Harrison Studio/D.P.I.; fig. 7-C © Karen Halverson/Omni-Photo Communications, Inc.; UNIT 8: fig. 8-A, Wide World Photos; fig. 8-B, Wide World Photos; fig. 8-C, Wide World Photos; UNIT 9: fig. 9-A, UPI; fig. 9-B, UPI, fig. 9-C, UPI; UNIT 10: fig. 10-A, The Granger Collection; fig. 10-B, The Granger Collection; fig. 10-C, The Granger Collection; UNIT 11: fig. 11-A, Wide World Photos; fig. 11-B, Wide World Photos; fig. 11-C, Wide World Photos; UNIT 12: fig. 12-A, Wide World Photos; fig. 12-B, Wide World Photos; fig. 12-C, Wide World Photos; UNIT 13: fig. 13-A, Wide World Photos; fig. 13-B, Wide World Photos; fig. 13-C, Wide World Photos; UNIT 14: fig. 14-A, Wide World Photos; fig. 14-B, © Lea/Omni-Photo Communications, Inc.; fig. 14-C, Wide World Photos; UNIT 15: fig. 15-A, © Jules Zalon/D.P.I.; fig. 15-B, © Lida Moser/D.P.I.; fig. 15-C, © Jules Zalon/D.P.I.

Printed in the United States of America   5 6 7 8 9 0

Authors

Sidney J. Rauch is Professor of Reading at Hofstra University, and senior author of the *World of Vocabulary* series. He has been a visiting professor at numerous universities and is active as a lecturer and consultant. As a member of the College Proficiency Examination Committee of the New York State Education Department, he is involved in the certification of reading personnel. He has given in-service courses and has served as consultant to over thirty school districts in New York, North Carolina, and South Carolina.

As coauthor and editor, his texts include *A Need to Read Series*, *Handbook for the Volunteer Tutor, Guiding the Reading Program, Mastering Reading Skills, Corrective Reading in the High School Classroom*, and the *Contained Reading Comprehension Series*. Dr. Rauch's many articles have appeared in *The Reading Teacher, Journal of Reading, Reading World*, and conference proceedings of the International Reading Association.

Alfred B. Weinstein is the former Principal of Myra S. Barnes Intermediate School (Staten Island, N.Y.). Dr. Weinstein has taught extensively at the secondary school level, and he has served as an elementary school principal and assistant principal. He has been a reading clinician and instructor at Hofstra University Reading Center. At Queens College, he gave courses in reading improvement, and at Brooklyn College he taught in the graduate teacher education program. Dr. Weinstein has also taught reading for the New York City Board of Education's in-service teacher training program. He was head of Unit 1 of the Board of Examiners and supervised the licensing of teachers, supervisors, administrators, psychologists, and social workers for the New York City Board of Education. He is a member of the staff of the Alfred Adler Mental Hygiene Clinic and teaches courses at the Alfred Adler Institute.

Dr. Weinstein is one of the authors of the Globe text *Achieving Reading Skills*. With Dr. Rauch, he is coauthor of *Mastering Reading Skills*.

Contents

1. Crossing the Atlantic

On August 17, 1978, three men landed their balloon, the Double Eagle II, on a field near Paris. They traveled over three thousand miles (4,828 kilometers) in their 112-foot (34-meter) balloon. They were in the air for six days. A record was set for distance traveled. These men were the first to cross the Atlantic by balloon.

The three heroes were Ben Abruzzo, Max Anderson, and Larry Newman. They are all from New Mexico. Abruzzo and Anderson had tried crossing the year before. They were forced to ditch near Iceland. But they didn't give up. They designed a new and more durable balloon.

Their historic flight began from the coast of Maine. The first few days were uneventful. Then a terrible thing happened. They dropped a few thousand feet in mid-air. But after that things got better. As they neared France, Anderson shouted, "We are on top of the world." When they landed they were mobbed by thousands of French people. It reminded the French of Charles Lindbergh's solo flight. America's honor rose to new heights in France and around the world.

Make a List

There are eight vocabulary words in this lesson. In the story, they are boxed in color. Copy the vocabulary words here.

1. _____   5. _____

2. _____   6. _____

3. _____   7. _____

4. _____   8. _____

3

Make an Alphabetical List

Here are the eight words you copied on the previous page. Write them in alphabetical order in the blank spaces below.

historic   honor   durable   solo
ditch   designed   mobbed   uneventful

1. _____   5. _____

2. _____   6. _____

3. _____   7. _____

4. _____   8. _____

What Do the Words Mean?

Here are some meanings for the eight vocabulary words in this lesson. Four words have been written beside their meanings. Write the other four words next to their meanings.

1. _____ long lasting; difficult to wear out

2. *uneventful* not exciting; ordinary

3. _____ famous in history; very important

4. *honor* good name; excellent reputation

5. _____ emergency landing; to land on water

6. *designed* planned; developed

7. *mobbed* surrounded by; crowded about

8. _____ to perform alone; to do by one's self

Phonics: Consonants

There are 26 letters in the alphabet. Twenty-one letters including the letter _y_ are called consonants. Five letters (_a_, _e_, _i_, _o_, _u_) and sometimes _y_ are called vowels.

Consonants appear at the beginning, at the end, and in the middle of words.

Consonants that appear in the middle are called medial consonants.

For example in the word *hammer*

    h   is a beginning consonant
    m is a medial consonant
    r   is a final consonant

Here are ten words. See how well you can recognize the beginning, medial, and final consonants. Each word in the list contains consonants. Some have beginning consonants. Some have medial consonants. Some have final consonants. Some may have all three types of consonants.

Check each word for all three consonant positions. Then write the consonants in each word in the correct list. The first one has been done as an example.

		Beginning	Medial	Final
1.	kitten	*k*	*tt*	*n*
2.	hoped			
3.	actor			
4.	corner			
5.	each			
6.	dancing			
7.	disco			
8.	umpire			
9.	tackle			
10.	action			

Find the Synonyms

A **synonym** is a word that means the same, or nearly the same, as another word. *Happy* and *glad* are synonyms.

The column on the left contains the eight key words in the story. To the right of each key word are three other words or groups of words. Two of these are synonyms for the key word. Circle the two synonyms.

1. ditch	crash landing	emergency landing	take off
2. solo	with friends	alone	without a companion
3. honor	regard	appearance	respect
4. uneventful	ordinary	exciting	usual
5. designed	flown	planned	developed
6. mobbed	surrounded by	ignored	crowded about
7. durable	strong	lasting	weak
8. historic	famous in history	important in history	uneventful in history

Using Your Language: Scrambled Sentences

These five sentences have been scrambled or mixed up. Write the words in the correct order so that they make complete sentences. The first one has been done as an example.

1. the Atlantic first the were to they cross

   They were the first to cross the Atlantic.

2. Eagle on the II Double field a landed

   _____

   _____

3. Mexico all balloonists three New were from

   _____

   _____

4. feet dropped 4,000 to balloon the 23,000 from feet

   _____

   _____

5. Lindbergh reminded Charles were the French of

   _____

   _____

Use Your Own Words _____

Look at the picture. What words come into your mind other than the ones you matched with their synonyms? Write them on the blank lines below. To help you get started, here are two good words:

1. *field* _____ 5. _____

2. *people* _____ 6. _____

3. _____ 7. _____

8

4. _____ 8. _____

Complete the Story _____

Here are the eight vocabulary words for this lesson:

historic   durable   solo   mobbed
honor   designed   uneventful   ditch

There are four blank spaces in the story below. Four vocabulary words have already been used in the story. They are underlined. Use the other four words to fill in the blank spaces.

It's good to know that there are still new worlds to conquer. Even in the 1980s there are large mountains to climb and wide oceans to cross. These _____ deeds will continue to bring honor to people of courage.

In the case of the three balloonists, the whole world watched and prayed. Many bad things could have happened. Ice could have formed and the balloonists might have had to ditch. Even though the balloon was designed to be _____ , a leak could have occurred.

After six days, the three balloonists landed in France. Their 3,100-mile (4,987-meter) trip was far from uneventful. They had set a record for distance. The world applauded. In France, they were _____ by cheering crowds. The French were reminded again of Lindbergh's _____ flight. It was a great moment for the three Americans.

2. Rebel in Rhythm

The spotlight is on Twyla Tharp and her dance company. She whirls like a top. The dancers tumble. They do this in rotation. While dancing they look like the blinking colors in a neon sign. Twyla moves with the speed of light. The audience cheers. Bouquets of flowers are tossed on stage in honor of a great performance.

Twyla Tharp, rebel of the dance, has made it. She's one of America's major choreographers (kor-ee-AG-ra-fers). Her job is to arrange the dances and direct the dancers. They only perform her works. Most of her dances are done on a plain stage with little scenery. The dancers usually wear very simple costumes. They perform their routines on gym floors, city streets, and parks.

Twyla combines jazz and classical music in her work. Sometimes she sets her dances to varied background music. But she doesn't always use music. Then all you hear are the dancers' breathing and the movements of their feet. She leaves all the rest up to your imagination.

Make a List

There are eight vocabulary words in this lesson. In the story, they are boxed in color. Copy the vocabulary words here.

1. _____   5. _____

2. _____   6. _____

3. _____   7. _____

4. _____   8. _____

Make an Alphabetical List _____

Here are the eight words you copied on the previous page. Write them in alphabetical order in the blank spaces below.

bouquets   rebel   background   routines
scenery   combines   rotation   major

1. _____   5. _____

2. _____   6. _____

3. _____   7. _____

4. _____   8. _____

What Do the Words Mean? _____

Here are some meanings for the eight vocabulary words in this lesson. Four words have been written beside their meanings. Write the other four words next to their meanings.

1. *rebel* _____ person who goes against the system; one who resists authority

2. _____ series of dance steps or movements

3. _____ bunches of flowers fastened together

4. *rotation* _____ taking turns in a regular order; one following the other

5. *scenery* _____ painted pictures or hangings for a stage

6. _____ joins together; mixes

7. *major* _____ important; principal

8. _____ past experience; events leading up to the present

Phonics: Long Vowels

It is important to know the vowels in the alphabet. They are _a_, _e_, _i_, _o_, _u_, and sometimes _y_.

When a vowel in a word has the same sound as its name, it is called a long vowel. The long vowel is marked by putting a line above the letter, like this: ā, ē, ī, ō, ū.

Here are two samples of each of the long vowels.

Long ā	**Long ē**	**Long ī**
cāke	wē	bīke
wāde	Pēte	fīre

Long ō	**Long ū**	**Sometimes ȳ**
drōve	mūsic	happȳ (long e sound)
grōw	hūman	crȳ (long i sound)

Look at the following words. Underline the words that have long vowel sounds and put a line above the long vowel. The first one has been done as an example.

tūbe   baby   store   pan   dime

flop   blew   made   ice   slow

Underline each word in parentheses that has a long vowel sound. Then draw a line above the long vowel. The first one has been done as an example.

1. Did you get that (glove, rōbe) for your birthday?

2. I (made, bought) a plane for my science class.

3. Lindbergh flew (swiftly, solo) across the Atlantic Ocean.

4. Would you like to be a (dancer, musician) one day?

5. Can you (ride, sit) on your horse?

6. I'll race you to the (lake, pond).

Find the Synonyms _____

A **synonym** is a word that means the same, or nearly the same, as another word. *Happy* and *glad* are synonyms.

The column on the left contains the eight key words in the story. To the right of each key word are three other words or groups of words. Two of these are synonyms for the key word. Circle the two synonyms.

1. bouquets	green plants	bunches of flowers	flowers tied together
2. combines	separates	joins	mixes
3. rotation	taking turns	speaking clearly	one after another
4. scenery	audience	stage pictures	stage hangings
5. background	future plans	past events	past history
6. major	principal	serious	important
7. routines	dance steps	dance histories	dance movements
8. rebel	one who acts against authority	one who joins the crowd	one who goes against the system

Using Your Language: Adjectives ───────

An **adjective** is a word that describes a person, place, or thing. For example, in the sentence "Twyla Tharp is a talented dancer," *talented* is the word which describes dancer. Underline the adjectives in the sentences below. The first one has been done as an example.

1. Twyla Tharp never expected to be a <u>famous</u> dancer.

2. Her dancers often perform on a bare stage with simple scenery.

3. After graduation, she continued studying with some of the best dance teachers.

4. A good dancer recognizes the value of an excellent teacher.

5. By combining jazz and classical ballet, Twyla has created exciting new dances.

Use Your Own Words

Look at the picture. What words come into your mind other than the ones you matched with their synonyms? Write them on the blank lines below. To help you get started, here are two good words:

1. *performers*   5. _____

2. *dancing*   6. _____

3. _____   7. _____

4. _____   8. _____

Complete the Story

Here are eight vocabulary words for this lesson:

rebel   routines   background   major
combines   rotation   scenery   bouquets

There are four blank spaces in the story below. Four vocabulary words have already been used in the story. They are underlined. Use the other four words to fill in the blank spaces.

Ballet has become an important art form in America. One of the people most responsible is Twyla Tharp. She has often been called a _____ because she does the unexpected. She <u>combines</u> jazz and classical ballet to form new _____. Sometimes she uses little or no <u>scenery</u> and no music. Her dancers perform unusual steps in <u>rotation</u>. They have been carefully trained by Twyla.

Twyla's _____ shows good training in dance and music. She studied musical instruments as well as most dance forms. She has also worked with some of the great dance teachers of our time.

Today, Twyla Tharp is known as one of America's _____ choreographers. A choreographer is a person who creates dance movements. Twyla's dances are often greeted with applause and <u>bouquets</u>. She has given pleasure to millions of dance lovers.

3. Batting Champion

For some athletes, fame comes quickly. For others, it is a long struggle. Rod Carew belongs to the latter group. Until the summer of 1977, he was nearly unknown. He had won the American League batting title five times. But people would still ask, "Rod who?" Then he made headlines. His photograph appeared on the cover of *Time* magazine. Fans began to recognize his skills. For most of the year, he was close to the .400 mark. That means for every ten times at bat, he got four hits. That's a very high batting average.

Rod was born in Panama in 1945. He came to this country in 1960. But he still remains a citizen of Panama. His good deeds on and off the field have brought fame to his birthplace. He is the only athlete to have received Panama's Medal of Honor.

Rod played for twelve seasons with the Minnesota Twins. Following the 1978 season, in which he won his seventh batting championship, he was traded to the California Angels. He continues to be a scientific hitter with few weaknesses. If anyone can reach the magic number of .400, Rod Carew seems to be a good candidate.

Make a List

There are eight vocabulary words in this lesson. In the story, they are boxed in color. Copy the vocabulary words here.

1. _____   5. _____

2. _____   6. _____

3. _____   7. _____

4. _____   8. _____

Make an Alphabetical List _____

Here are the eight words you copied on the previous page. Write them in alphabetical order in the blank spaces below.

struggle	deeds	candidate	headlines
latter	scientific	average	photograph

1. _____   5. _____

2. _____   6. _____

3. _____   7. _____

4. _____   8. _____

What Do the Words Mean? _____

Here are some meanings for the eight vocabulary words in this lesson. Four words have been written beside their meanings. Write the other four words next to their meanings.

1. *photograph*   picture taken by a camera

2. _____   hard battle; a fight

3. *average*   a mathematical term used to show how well a batter is doing

4. _____   acts; things done

5. _____   person who has been named or proposed for an award or position

6. *latter*   the last of two things mentioned

7. _____   lines in large type at the top of a newspaper or article

8. *scientific*   done with much thought or knowledge; exact

20

Phonics: Short Vowels

It is also important to know the short vowel sounds. Remember, the vowels are *a, e, i, o, u,* and sometimes *y.*

Below are some words that contain the short vowel sounds. Look at them carefully and say them slowly. Stretch out the sounds so you can hear the vowels.

You will notice when there is just one vowel in a word, it has the short sound. A short vowel is marked by putting a small curved mark—ŭ—above the letter.

Here are two samples of each of the short vowels.

short ă	short ĕ	short ĭ	short ŏ	short ŭ
măt	lĕt	fĭt	ŏx	ŭp
băttle	bĕd	fĭddle	bŏttle	ŭnder

Underline each word in parentheses that has a short vowel sound. Then draw a ˘ above the short vowel. The first one has been done as an example.

1. The ambulance parked near (Fay's, Jăck's) house.

2. I heard birds (scolding, chattering) in their nest.

3. I have two (mice, kittens). Do you want to see them?

4. My dog plays many (tricks, jokes) on me.

5. His (coat, fur) is falling out.

6. The scout master always uses a (ruler, branch) to point the way.

Find the Synonyms

A **synonym** is a word that means the same, or nearly the same; as another word. *Happy* and *glad* are synonyms.

The column on the left contains the eight key words in the story. To the right of each key word are three other words or groups of words. Two of these are synonyms for the key word. Circle the two synonyms.

1. candidate	person	award	individual
2. photograph	picture	image	painting
3. average	baseball term	low score	math term
4. latter	last in order	former	second of two
5. scientific	systematic	exact	messy
6. deeds	thoughts	acts	things done
7. struggle	conflict	battle	medal
8. headlines	words at the head of an article	words under a picture	large print at the top of a newspaper

Using Your Language: Capital Letters _____

In each of the following sentences there are words which require capital letters. Rewrite each sentence so the words are correctly capitalized. Remember that capital letters are used in the following places: first word in a sentence; names of people, cars, cities, states, countries, days of the week, months of the year. The first sentence has been done as an example.

1. rod carew, won his seventh american league batting championship.

Rod Carew, won his seventh American league batting Championship.

2. you can tell that rod carew is famous when he is compared to people like ted williams, stan musial, and ty cobb.

_____

_____

_____

3. rod carew's photograph has appeared on the cover of *time, newsweek* ,and *sports illustrated*.

_____

_____

_____

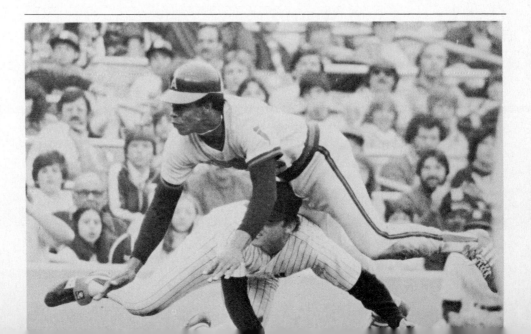

Use Your Own Words ————————————

Look at the picture. What words come into your mind other than the ones you matched with their synonyms? Write them on the blank lines below. To help you get started, here are two good words:

1. *uniform*   5. _____

2. *player*   6. _____

3. _____   7. _____

4. _____   8. _____

Complete the Story

Here are the eight vocabulary words for this lesson:

struggle   deeds   photograph   average
latter   scientific   candidate   headlines

There are four blank spaces in the story below. Four vocabulary words have already been used in the story. They are underlined. Use the other four words to fill in the blank spaces.

There have been many famous batting champions in baseball. Some great hitters immediately come to mind: Babe Ruth, Ty Cobb, and Ted Williams. The <u>latter</u> was the last player to hit over .400. Now there is a new figure making <u>headlines</u>. His name is Rod Carew, and he is a citizen of Panama. Fame did not come quickly to Rod. It was a very long _____ before people recognized his skills. Rod practiced hard. He studied other batters. He made a <u>scientific</u> study of hitting. As a result, his batting _____ led the league for seven years. When he won his seventh batting championship in 1978, his _____ appeared in many newspapers and magazines.

Rod is more than a famous player. He is a thoughtful citizen on and off the field. His good <u>deeds</u> have made him a national hero. In Panama he is so popular, he probably would be a good _____ for president.

4. The Strongest Woman in the World

You have heard of great athletes. But women power lifters? That's another story. There's a young lady in Nova Scotia who is changing the records. Her name is Jan Todd. She is the holder of three world records in lifting. At a recent meet, she lifted over 1,000 pounds in three events. The total was 100 pounds more than any woman had ever lifted. These were all tests of pure muscle strength.

Who is this young woman who is being hailed as the "world's strongest"? Jan Todd is an attractive blonde. She weighs 170 pounds. She was always a natural athlete. But power lifting never entered her mind. That is, not until she met her future husband Terry Todd. Terry was a professor at a university. He was also a former record-holder in power lifting. Jan became interested in the sport while watching her husband at practice. Then she went through four years of serious training. As a result she became the best.

Why does she do it? Why does she undergo the physical strain of lifting? Jan explains, "I lift because I love it. I love the way it makes me feel. It has extended my idea of the limits of what is possible for me."

Make a List _____

There are eight vocabulary words in this lesson. In the story, they are boxed in color. Copy the vocabulary words here.

1._____   5._____

2._____   6._____

3._____   7._____

4._____   8._____

27

Make an Alphabetical List _____

Here are the eight words you copied on the previous
page. Write them in alphabetical order in the blank
spaces below.

professor	hailed	natural	total
undergo	attractive	muscle	limits

1. _____   5. _____

2. _____   6. _____

3. _____   7. _____

4. _____   8. _____

What Do the Words Mean? _____

Here are some meanings for the eight vocabulary words
in this lesson. Four words have been written beside their
meanings. Write the other four words next to their
meanings.

1. _____ a teacher, usually in a college or
university; a learned person

2. *hailed* named with pride; called; saluted

3. _____ tissue made of cells or fibers

4. *limits* boundary lines; borders

5. *total* sum; entire amount

6. _____ qualities or skills that a person is
born with

7. _____ pretty; pleasing; charming

8. *undergo* to go through; to experience

Phonics: Digraphs _____

Digraphs are two consonants or vowels that make a single sound. They can appear at the beginning, middle, and end of words. In this lesson, you will work with beginning consonant digraphs.

Here are some examples of beginning consonant digraphs.

ch	**sh**	**kn**	**th**	**wh**	**wr**
chicken	shine	knew	thin	when	wrong
child	shoe	knife	this	where	write

The following sentences contain incomplete words that can be completed by using a beginning consonant digraph. Read each sentence carefully. Decide which of the digraphs listed above is needed for each underlined word. Then write the digraphs next to each incomplete word. The first one has been done as an example.

1. The wagon won't work because a *wh* eel came off.

2. How do you like my new gold _____ ain?

3. Did your dog catch the ball you _____ rew?

4. My toes hurt because my _____ oes are too tight.

5. _____ ree is my lucky number. Do you _____ ow yours?

6. No matter how I try to put my lips together, I still can't _____ istle.

7. The coffee will stay hot if you pour it into a _____ ermos.

8. They went to Sunday morning _____ urch services.

9. As a result of five _____ ong answers, he failed the test.

10. Do you know the story of Moby Dick, the _____ ite _____ ale?

29

Find the Synonyms

A **synonym** is a word that means the same, or nearly the same, as another word. *Happy* and *glad* are synonyms.

The column on the left contains the eight key words in the story. To the right of each key word are three other words or groups of words. Two of these are synonyms for the key word. Circle the two synonyms.

1. total	entire amount	width	sum
2. natural	man-made	born with	inborn
3. undergo	go through	avoid	experience
4. hailed	called	saluted	carried
5. professor	student	teacher	learned person
6. attractive	pretty	ordinary	charming
7. limits	borders	designs	boundaries
8. muscle	bone	body tissue	cells that contract

Using Your Language: Check Your Spelling _____

There are many words in our language that are often misspelled. These words are spelled incorrectly so many times that they are sometimes called *spelling demons*. (Note: a demon is a devil or evil spirit—and these words cause a great deal of trouble.) Here are some words that cause trouble. There is a correct spelling and an incorrect one. Underline the correct spelling. Then write out each correct word on the blank lines. The first one has been done as an example.

		Correct Spelling
<u>receive</u>	recieve	*receive*
alright	all right	_____
pleasant	pleasent	_____
certain	certin	_____
calendir	calendar	_____
benefit	benifit	_____
discribe	describe	_____

Use Your Own Words

Look at the picture. What words come into your mind other than the ones you matched with their synonyms? Write them on the blank lines below. To help you get started, here are two good words:

1. _woman_   5. _____
2. _jacket_   6. _____
3. _____   7. _____
4. _____   8. _____

Complete the Story

Here are the eight vocabulary words for this lesson:

professor   hailed   natural   total
undergo   attractive   muscle   limits

There are four blank spaces in the story below. Four vocabulary words have already been used in the story. They are underlined. Use the other four words to fill in the blank spaces.

Records are made to be broken. That's one reason why an <u>attractive</u> 5'7" woman keeps practicing. Before her next meet she will _____ months of serious training. She will exercise daily and watch her diet. Before the big event, she will work to the <u>limits</u> of her ability.

Power lifting is a test of almost pure _____ strength. All the training in the world will not make a champion unless the strength is there. Jan Todd was always a _____ athlete. She could run and throw with the best. She became interested in power lifting when she met her future husband. He was a university <u>professor</u> and a former record-holder.

Today, Jan and Terry Todd practice together. They are both teachers who enjoy working with youngsters and adults. They add to their _____ income by raising cattle. Jan knows that power lifting is a great strain on her body. But not everyone has the honor of being <u>hailed</u> as the "world's strongest."

5. High Flyer

At the age of 14, Tito Gaona saw a movie. It changed his life. The movie was *Trapeze* with Burt Lancaster and Tony Curtis. Tony played an aerialist who wanted to do the "triple." The triple is three somersaults in mid-air off a swinging trapeze. This movie inspired Tito. He made up his mind to become a trapeze artist.

He practiced with his father, Vincent, a former acrobat. Vincent became his "catcher." The catcher is the person who grasps the flyer as he completes the movements. At the age of 18, Tito was doing the triple in the circus. Only four persons had done the triple before Tito. Two of them died from broken necks while performing.

During the stunt, Tito moves at an incredible speed. He travels at 75 miles (120 kilometers) an hour. If Tito lands on his neck, he could break it. He has only a fraction of a second to tuck his neck in. Then he has to land on his back in the net.

One day Tito completed the "quadruple." His catcher caught him. But it was just practice. That was the problem. There were no cameras or spectators to see him do it. Some day, he'll do it under "The Big Top" and thousands will be watching.

Make a List

There are eight vocabulary words in this lesson. In the story, they are boxed in color. Copy the vocabulary words here.

1. _____   5. _____

2. _____   6. _____

3. _____   7. _____

4. _____   8. _____

35

Make an Alphabetical List _____

Here are the eight words you copied on the previous page. Write them in alphabetical order in the blank spaces below.

| trapeze | tuck | somersaults | stunt |
| acrobat | aerialist | fraction | incredible |

1. _____   5. _____

2. _____   6. _____

3. _____   7. _____

4. _____   8. _____

What Do the Words Mean? _____

Here are some meanings for the eight vocabulary words in this lesson. Four words have been written beside their meanings. Write the other four words next to their meanings.

1. *aerialist*   a person who performs on a trapeze; a flyer

2. _____   acrobatic stunts; full body turns, forward or backward

3. *tuck*   to pull in; draw in closely

4. _____   daring trick; display of skill

5. *fraction*   small part; less than a second in time

6. _____   short horizontal bar, hung by two ropes, on which aerialists perform

7. *acrobat*   skilled gymnast; expert in tumbling

8. _____   almost impossible to believe; highly unusual

Once again, let's look at some words that have short vowel sounds. For example, *cap, hop, rip*. Now add *e* to each of these words. Look at the new words: *cape, hope, ripe*. Notice that each of the new words now has the *long* vowel in the middle and the final *e* is silent.

Here is a list of words containing the short vowel sound. Make new words by adding an *e* to the end of each word. Then write the new words on the lines provided. Pronounce each new word to yourself. It should have the long vowel sound. The first one has been done as an example.

cop _*cape*_____

pip _____

past _____

pan _____

dim _____

slop _____

cub _____

kit _____

mad _____

bit _____

hug _____

strip _____

cut _____

fad _____

hop _____

pin _____

rat _____

rid _____

spin _____

Find the Synonyms _____

A **synonym** is a word that means the same, or nearly the same, as another word. *Happy* and *glad* are synonyms.

The column on the left contains the eight key words in the story. To the right of each key word are three other words or groups of words. Two of these are synonyms for the key word. Circle the two synonyms.

1. incredible	amazing	unbelievable	ordinary
2. somersaults	circus food	acrobatic tricks	full body turns
3. tuck	unfold	pull in	draw together
4. aerialist	circus flyer	ring-master	performer on a trapeze
5. stunt	clever trick	stupid idea	daring feat
6. acrobat	expert gymnast	skilled tumbler	animal trainer
7. trapeze	circular cage	a swing for aerialists	bar hung from two ropes
8. fraction	small part	tiny piece	total thing

Using Your Language: Word Endings ———

Many words end in *ed, er,* or *ing.* These endings are called suffixes. A **suffix** can change the meaning of a word or form a new word. Add the correct suffix to the word before each sentence. Then write the new word in the blank space. Remember, sometimes you drop the final *e* before adding the *ed, er,* or *ing.* The first one has been done as an example.

1. tuck   He ____*tucked*____ his neck in before hitting the net.

2. catch   The _____ must grasp the aerialist's forearms.

3. watch   Some day he will succeed and thousands will be _____.

4. move   The aerialist is _____ through the air at an incredible speed.

5. complete   To date, no one has _____ the quadruple in public.

6. change   The movie *Trapeze* _____ his life.

7. announce   The _____ asked the crowd to be quiet.

8. somersault   Maria felt like a new person as she _____ through the air.

Use Your Own Words

Look at the picture. What words come into your mind other than the ones you matched with their synonyms? Write them on the blank lines below. To help you get started, here are two good words:

1. *wires*   5. _____
2. *flying*   6. _____
3. _____   7. _____
4. _____   8. _____

Complete the Story

Here are the eight vocabulary words for this lesson:

aerialist   tuck   stunt   acrobat
trapeze   incredible   somersaults   fraction

There are four blank spaces in the story below. Four vocabulary words have already been used in the story. They are underlined. Use the other four words to fill in the blank spaces.

There are many popular circus acts. Each has its own special appeal. But when an aerialist starts to climb to the _____, all the other acts stop. These high flyers become the center of all eyes. Even though there is a net below, the risk is still there. Flying through the air at _____ speed does not allow for errors. A failure to tuck in one's head can cause serious injury.

One of the most amazing performers is Tito Gaona. He has made the "triple" a regular part of his act. Now he is working on the "quadruple." It is not just an ordinary stunt. This involves four back _____ in mid-air. Only the most skilled acrobat could think of trying it. It requires skill, strength, and timing. If the flyer is only a _____ off the mark, it can mean a rough tumble to the net — and more practice!

Nobel Prize Winner

Rosalyn Yalow is the second woman to win the Nobel Prize in medicine. She's a scientist from New York City. She works eighty hours a week. Rosalyn feels she must work harder than men to succeed. She says, "It's a man's world." But she's trying to change that.

Rosalyn worked out a way to measure substances in the blood and tissue. It doesn't matter how small the substance is. Her method can measure it. This finding helps detect disease early.

In college Rosalyn had high honors in science. After college she applied for a job as a teaching aid. But she was turned down. Rosalyn was rejected because she was a woman. Even after this defeat she was resolved to win. She said, "I'm going to show the world a woman can succeed."

Finally the University of Illinois admitted her to medical school. Rosalyn worked and studied there until graduation. Then she returned to New York where jobs were plentiful. Rosalyn got a job in a hospital. There she started doing research to help people. That was 31 years ago. She's still there today working to discover more cures for disease.

Rosalyn Yalow, super scientist, is a super woman!

Make a List

There are eight vocabulary words in this lesson. In the story, they are boxed in color. Copy the vocabulary words here.

1. _____   5. _____

2. _____   6. _____

3. _____   7. _____

4. _____   8. _____

Make an Alphabetical List _____

Here are the eight words you copied on the previous page. Write them in alphabetical order in the blank spaces below.

admitted   detect   succeed   research
substances   resolved   plentiful   rejected

1. _____   5. _____

2. _____   6. _____

3. _____   7. _____

4. _____   8. _____

What Do the Words Mean? _____

Here are some meanings for the eight vocabulary words in this lesson. Four words have been written beside their meanings. Write the other four words next to their meanings.

1. *detect* _____ to discover; to find out

2. _____ to reach a desired goal

3. *research* _____ careful study of some field of knowledge; investigation

4. _____ materials from which something is made

5. *resolved* _____ determined; fixed in purpose

6. _____ refused or turned away

7. *plentiful* _____ more than enough; abundant

8. _____ given permission to enroll as a student; allowed to enter

Phonics: Blends ───────────────────────

Blends are the sounds of two or three consonants that come together at the beginning, middle, or end of words. You will study some beginning blends in this lesson.

Here are some examples of beginning consonant blends:

bl	**br**	**cl**	**cr**	**dr**
blend	brag	clown	crook	drop

fl	**gr**	**spr**	**str**
flag	grass	spread	stroke

Complete the following sentences by supplying a word that begins with a consonant blend. For example, "The synonym for *happy* is _____." The answer must begin with a blend. The answer is *glad*. The first one has been done as an example.

1. One of the *blades* _____ on her new pair of skates was bent.

2. He tried to catch the mouse in his new _____.

3. A word that means the opposite of back is _____.

4. A farmer plants seeds to get a _____.

5. A circus comic is called a _____.

6. The picture was too small for the _____.

7. Before you mail a letter, make sure it has a _____.

8. She felt so pretty in her new _____.

9. After the race, he looked forward to a big _____ of cold milk.

10. Our English _____ ended early today.

Find the Synonyms _____

A **synonym** is a word that means the same, or nearly the same, as another word. *Happy* and *glad* are synonyms.

The column on the left contains the eight key words in the story. To the right of each key word are three other words or groups of words. Two of these are synonyms for the key word. Circle the two synonyms.

1. research	careful study	motion	investigation
2. detect	find out	hate	discover
3. rejected	lost	turned away	refused
4. succeed	do well	fail	reach a goal
5. plentiful	few	more than enough	a great many
6. admitted	accepted	refused	allowed in
7. substances	materials	matter	thoughts
8. resolved	changed	decided	determined

Using Your Language: Antonyms

Antonyms are words that are opposite in meaning. For example, *good* and *bad*, and *fast* and *slow* are antonyms. Here are antonyms for six of the vocabulary words. See if you can find the vocabulary words, and write them in the blank spaces on the left. The first one has been done as an example.

Vocabulary Word	Antonym
1. *resolved*	undecided
2. _____	fail
3. _____	scarce
4. _____	accepted
5. _____	refused entrance
6. _____	careless study

47

Use Your Own Words _____

Look at the picture. What words come into your mind other than the ones you matched with their synonyms? Write them on the blank lines below. To help you get started, here are two good words:

1. *handshake*   5. _____

2. *medals*   6. _____

3. _____   7. _____

48

4. _____   8. _____

Complete the Story _____

Here are the eight vocabulary words for this lesson:

succeed   detect   resolved   admitted
research   rejected   substances   plentiful

There are four blank spaces in the story below. Four vocabulary words have already been used in the story. They are underlined. Use the other four words to fill in the blank spaces.

Marie Curie was the first woman to win the Nobel Prize for her <u>research</u> in medicine. That happened in 1911. Sixty-six years later, the prize was awarded to Rosalyn Yalow. She had found a new way of measuring _____ in the blood. Any discovery that can <u>detect</u> disease early deserves a prize. Many lives have been saved because of Rosalyn Yalow's work.

Rosalyn came from a poor family. But her parents _____ that their daughter would have a better life. They knew the importance of education. Rosalyn never forgot their advice. She was determined to <u>succeed</u>.

After college Rosalyn applied to many universities to be a teaching aid. She was <u>rejected</u> because she was a woman. Finally the University of Illinois _____ her. Later she returned to New York for a job. They were _____ at that time. She went to work in a hospital. Today she is still there studying and working to help overcome disease.

7. walking the high steel

"Look out! Steel beam coming up!" the foreman called. Jim Tallchief climbed the steel structure with the skill of a cat. Quickly, he worked his way from beam to beam. He balanced himself with ease. Jim was alert. He grasped the rising beam and fastened it in place.

Jim Tallchief is a Mohawk. He is proud of his Indian ancestors. They are famous for being surefooted. Mohawks are the most agile steelworkers in the world. Much of their labor is done in small groups. The work is very dangerous. So it is important that they cooperate with one another. Each member of the group must know that his co-workers will be alert under pressure.

In 1907, a bridge collapsed before it was finished. It caused the death of 35 Mohawks. Strangely enough, the risk made the work more attractive to some of the Indians. But their wives insisted that large groups of men no longer work on the same construction project. They felt that many women could become widows through one accident.

The life of a steelworker is hard. The men are proud of their deeds. They feel that to excel on the high beam is to prove one's self as an Indian and as a man.

Make a List

There are eight vocabulary words in this lesson. In the story, they are boxed in color. Copy the vocabulary words here.

1. _____   5. _____

2. _____   6. _____

3. _____   7. _____

4. _____   8. _____

Make an Alphabetical List _____

Here are the eight words you copied on the previous page. Write them in alphabetical order in the blank spaces below.

alert   collapsed   widows   foreman
construction   agile   skill   ease

1. _____   5. _____

2. _____   6. _____

3. _____   7. _____

4. _____   8. _____

What Do the Words Mean? _____

Here are some meanings for the eight vocabulary words in this lesson. Four words have been written beside their meanings. Write the other four words next to their meanings.

1. _____   broke down suddenly; fell down

2. *alert* _____   quick in thought and action; watchful

3. _____   the process of building

4. *widows* _____   women whose husbands have died

5. _____   having quick, easy movements; limber

6. *skill* _____   ability to use one's knowledge in doing something

7. _____   person in charge of a group of workers; a boss

8. *ease* _____   natural way or manner

Phonics: Syllables _____

Words have rhythm. They are divided into syllables like musical beats in a song or dance.

If you understand syllables, your spelling and pronunciation will improve. Say the following words slowly and clap for each syllable as you say them. For example:

climb	=	one syllable
climb ing	=	two syllables
po ta to	=	three syllables
im poss i ble	=	four syllables

Here is a short rule to keep in mind.
For each syllable, there must be a *vowel sound.*

Look at the following list of words. Write the number of vowels in each word. Then say the word, and listen for the number of vowel sounds. The number of vowel sounds you hear will be the number of syllables in the word. For example, in the word *tried* there are two vowels, *i* and *e*. However, there is only one vowel sound—the long *i*. Therefore, there is only one syllable. The first one has been done as an example.

Word	Number of Vowels	Number of Vowel Sounds	Number of Syllables
drive	2	1	1
hockey			
microfilm			
motorcycle			
football			
track			
basketball			
runner			
janitor			

Find the Synonyms _____

A **synonym** is a word that means the same, or nearly the same, as another word. *Happy* and *glad* are synonyms.

The column on the left contains the eight key words in the story. To the right of each key word are three other words or groups of words. Two of these are synonyms for the key word. Circle the two synonyms.

1. foreman	boss	assistant	person in charge
2. skill	ability	knowledge	fear
3. ease	comfort	stress	relaxation
4. alert	lazy	watchful	quick in thought
5. collapsed	gave way	fell down	held together
6. construction	process of building	style of painting	manner of building
7. agile	coordinated	clumsy	quick
8. widows	women who have lost their husbands through death	divorced women	women whose husbands have died

Using Your Language: Words Often Confused _____

Some words are often confused because they look alike or sound alike. For example, *there* and *their,* and *where* and *wear* are often confused. Place the correct word in each of the blank spaces in the following sentences. The first one has been done as an example.

1. (picture, pitcher)   In my baseball scrapbook, I have a *picture* _____ of my favorite *pitcher* _____.

2. (lose, loose)   Since my top button is _____ , I will probably _____ it.

3. (wait, weight)   The woman had to _____ in line before the doctor could check her _____ .

4. (would, wood)   If we start chopping now, we _____ have enough _____ for the entire winter.

5. (passed, past)   For the _____ three years, I have _____ every examination that has come my way.

6. (meat, meet)   Tell your mother, I will _____ her in front of the _____ counter.

Use Your Own Words

Look at the picture. What words come into your mind other than the ones you matched with their synonyms? Write them on the blank lines below. To help you get started, here are two good words:

1. *water*
2. *height*
3. _____
4. _____

5. _____
6. _____
7. _____
8. _____

Complete the Story _____

Here are the eight vocabulary words for this lesson:

widows   agile   skill   ease
construction   foreman   collapsed   alert

There are four blank spaces in the story below. Four vocabulary words have already been used in the story. They are underlined. Use the other four words to fill in the blank spaces.

Steelworkers are a special breed. It takes unusual skill and courage to walk the high beams. If one is not alert, lives may be in danger. Among the most _____ steelworkers are the Mohawk Indians. They have been doing this work for many years. When a high bridge is under construction, the _____ looks for Mohawk workers. He knows he can rely on them. They are surefooted and dependable. They cooperate with ease.

Work on the high beams is not without great loss. In 1907, a bridge _____ and caused the deaths of 35 Mohawks. This disaster did not stop the others from working. But their wives insisted that large numbers of men no longer work on the same project. They couldn't afford to lose too many of their brave men. There were far too many _____ already.

8. By Popular Demand

A music critic called Anne Murray "a princess with taste and style." That's an accurate picture of her. She has the charm and beauty that wins an audience. When she sings a love song the lyrics come alive. Anne Murray attracts a wide following. She can sing country, pop, or jazz. As Anne says, "I'm not limited to one style. I have a lot of confidence in my singing. I put a great deal of work into my music."

Anne was born in Canada. She was raised in the coal mining town of Springhill, Nova Scotia. After graduation she taught for a year. Then Anne did some singing on Canadian television. Her first big international hit was "Snowbird." She became the first female Canadian recording artist to get a gold in the United States. Since then she has become a favorite concert attraction. For five straight years she won the "Best Female Vocalist" award in Canada. And in 1979, Anne Murray was named "Best Female Pop Vocalist" at the twenty-first annual Grammy Awards.

Her album "Let's Keep It That Way" was a big hit. It contained many warm and tender love songs. One critic said it was "an exceptional offering from a truly fine artist." Now when Anne Murray appears in concert, it is always "by popular demand."

Make a List

There are eight vocabulary words in this lesson. In the story, they are boxed in color. Copy the vocabulary words here.

1. _____
2. _____
3. _____
4. _____
5. _____
6. _____
7. _____
8. _____

59

Make an Alphabetical List

Here are the eight words you copied on the previous page. Write them in alphabetical order in the blank spaces below.

concert   limited   international   tender
vocalist   demand   accurate   exceptional

1. _____   5. _____

2. _____   6. _____

3. _____   7. _____

4. _____   8. _____

What Do the Words Mean?

Here are some meanings for the eight vocabulary words in this lesson. Four words have been written beside their meanings. Write the other four words next to their meanings.

1. _____ gentle; sensitive

2. *exceptional* way above the average; excellent

3. _____ one who sings; singer

4. *demand* ask for; request

5. _____ involving two or more nations

6. *limited* kept within certain boundaries; restricted

7. _____ musical performance

8. *accurate* correct; careful and exact

Phonics: Compound Words_____

When you join one whole word with another whole word, a new single word is formed. This new word is called a compound word.

For example, when you put the two words *air* and *plane* together, you get *airplane*. Here are three more examples.

> steam + ship = steamship
> bed   + room = bedroom
> cow   + boy   = cowboy

Draw lines from Column A to Column B to form new compound words. The first one has been done as an example.

A	B
head	stick
wish	lines
drum	store
bath	ache
stomach	cut
news	bone
drug	paper
hair	tub
boy	ball
base	sick
some	be
home	nut
may	time
pea	scout

Find the Synonyms _____

A **synonym** is a word that means the same, or nearly the same, as another word. *Happy* and *glad* are synonyms.

The column on the left contains the eight key words in the story. To the right of each key word are three other words or groups of words. Two of these are synonyms for the key word. Circle the two synonyms.

1. international	among nations	concerning countries	within one nation
2. concert	musical show	funny act	musical performance
3. demand	refuse	request	ask
4. tender	gentle	rough	loving
5. vocalist	singer	dancer	songstress
6. exceptional	very good	ordinary	above average
7. accurate	uneven	exact	correct
8. limited	open	within boundaries	confined

Using Your Language: Contractions _____

Many times two words are shortened into one by leaving out one or more letters and putting in an apostrophe. The shortened word is called a **contraction.** For example, *I'll* is the contraction for *I will. Don't* is the contraction for *do not.* In the left hand column are the two words that form the contraction. Write the contraction in the right hand column. The first one has been done as an example.

	Contraction
they are	*they're*
can not	_____
does not	_____
who is	_____
you have	_____
it is	_____
you will	_____
have not	_____

Use Your Own Words ———————————

Look at the picture. What words come into your mind other than the ones you matched with their synonyms? Write them on the blank lines below. To help you get started, here are two good words:

1. *microphone*   5. _____

2. *lights*   6. _____

3. _____   7. _____

64

4. _____   8. _____

Complete the Story ─────────────

Here are the eight vocabulary words for this lesson:

international   concert   demand   tender
vocalist   exceptional accurate   limited

There are four blank spaces in the story below. Four vocabulary words have already been used in the story. They are underlined. Use the other four words to fill in the blank spaces.

At the beginning of her career, Anne Murray's fame was <u>limited</u> to Canada. She was often called "Canada's sweetheart." She won that country's "Best Female _____" award five times. Then came her first big <u>international</u> hit, "Snowbird." Other hit records followed. She appeared on top television shows in Canada and the United States. She became a popular _____ attraction throughout North America. When she performed, it was usually by popular <u>demand</u>.

How did Anne Murray get so far? There are many answers. She has beauty, charm, and a lovely voice. She can sing many types of songs. She is especially good with _____ love songs. But most of all, she is willing to word hard to improve her act. Her album "Let's Keep It That Way" was called really "<u>exceptional</u>" by one critic. It would be _____ to say that her future albums will be even better.

9. The Grey Cup

The United States has its Super Bowl. Canada has the Grey Cup. Both games are lively. Without debating the good points of each, the Grey Cup arouses more interest. The whole country takes part. It is more than a game. People celebrate. It is a mixture of Mardi Gras and New Year's Eve.

The title game is played alternately in Montreal and Toronto. These cities have large stadiums. And they also have the best weather for the game. Some people call the Grey Cup, "The Arctic ancestor of the Super Bowl."

The Grey Cup was given by Lord Grey. It has become the main trophy of Canadian football. At first, the cup was to go to the winner of the amateur football title. Then the cup was changed to a professional award. Some American players have been imported to play for Canadian teams.

The rivalry between East and West is intense. The Montreal Alouettes won the Grey Cup in 1970, '74, and '77. But the Edmonton Eskimos avenged the losses in 1978 and '79. The competition is strong. But it continues to make the Grey Cup a matter of national interest in Canada.

Make a List

There are eight vocabulary words in this lesson. In the story, they are boxed in color. Copy the vocabulary words here.

1. _____   5. _____

2. _____   6. _____

3. _____   7. _____

4. _____   8. _____

Make an Alphabetical List _____

Here are the eight words you copied on the previous page. Write them in alphabetical order in the blank spaces below.

mixture   trophy   arouses   avenged
imported   debating   alternately   intense

1. _____   5. _____

2. _____   6. _____

3. _____   7. _____

4. _____   8. _____

What Do the Words Mean? _____

Here are some meanings for the eight vocabulary words in this lesson. Four words have been written beside their meanings. Write the other four words next to their meanings.

1. _____   a prize, usually a silver cup

2. *arouses*   stirs up strong feelings; awakens

3. _____   combination; something made up by mixing two or more things

4. *imported*   brought into a country

5. *intense*   very strong; severe

6. _____   discussing opposing reasons; arguing

7. _____   took revenge; got even

  8. *alternately*   taking turns; first one, then the other

Phonics: Prefixes

Prefixes are one or more letters attached to the beginning of a word. Prefixes have different meanings. When they join words, they change the meaning of the word. There are many prefixes in our language. A few will be discussed in this lesson. For example:

pre	means *before*
pre	+ cook = precook (to cook before)
super	means *more than, extra*
super	+ man = superman (extra special man)
un	means *not* or *the opposite of*
un	+ happy = unhappy (not happy)

In the following list connect the prefix with the root word. Write the new word and its meaning on the lines provided. The first one has been done as an example.

Prefix	Root Word	New Word
un (not or opposite)	+ real	= *unreal*
super (extra, great)	+ highway	= _____
pre (before)	+ paid	= _____
dis (not)	+ honest	= _____
re (again or back)	+ turn	= _____
in (not)	+ complete	= _____
sub (under, below)	+ marine	= _____

69

Find the Synonyms _____

A **synonym** is a word that means the same, or nearly the same, as another word. *Happy* and *glad* are synonyms.

The column on the left contains the eight key words in the story. To the right of each key word are three other words or groups of words. Two of these are synonyms for the key word. Circle the two synonyms.

1. mixture	combination	discovery	blend
2. imported	sent out	brought in	taken in
3. debating	arguing	discussing	ignoring
4. alternately	two at a time	taking turns	one after the other
5. intense	very strong	dull	sharp
6. arouses	awakens	stirs up	calms
7. avenged	took revenge	cheated	got even
8. trophy	sad event	winning prize	silver cup

Using Your Language: Describe the Nouns

Two of the words used in the story, *trophy* and *mixture,* are nouns. Think of the trophies and mixtures you have seen or read about. What words can you use to describe them? List as many adjectives as you can which tell something about these nouns. The list has been started for you.

trophy

1. *silver*
2. *magnificent*
3. _____
4. _____
5. _____
6. _____
7. _____
8. _____

mixture

1. *attractive*
2. *interesting*
3. _____
4. _____
5. _____
6. _____
7. _____
8. _____

Use Your Own Words

Look at the picture. What words come into your mind other than the ones you matched with their synonyms? Write them on the blank lines below. To help you get started, here are two good words:

1. *football*
2. *game*
3.
4.

5.
6.
7.
8.

Complete the Story _____

Here are the eight vocabulary words for this lesson:

trophy   arouses   debating   alternately
avenged   imported   intense   mixture

There are four blank spaces in the story below. Four vocabulary words have already been used in the story. They are underlined. Use the other four words to fill in the blank spaces.

In the United States, the Super Bowl is a major event. In Canada, the Grey Cup arouses even more excitement. This football game is held _____ in Toronto and Montreal. These great cities can handle the large crowds. For weeks before the game, much time is spent debating the quality of the teams. No one tries to hide the _____ rivalry between the teams involved.

The Grey Cup has produced outstanding games over the years. Montreal and Edmonton were the rivals in 1977 and 1978. Montreal won the _____ in 1977; Edmonton avenged the defeat in 1978. In both games, _____ players from American colleges played key roles. This mixture of Canadian and American players gives the game an added interest.

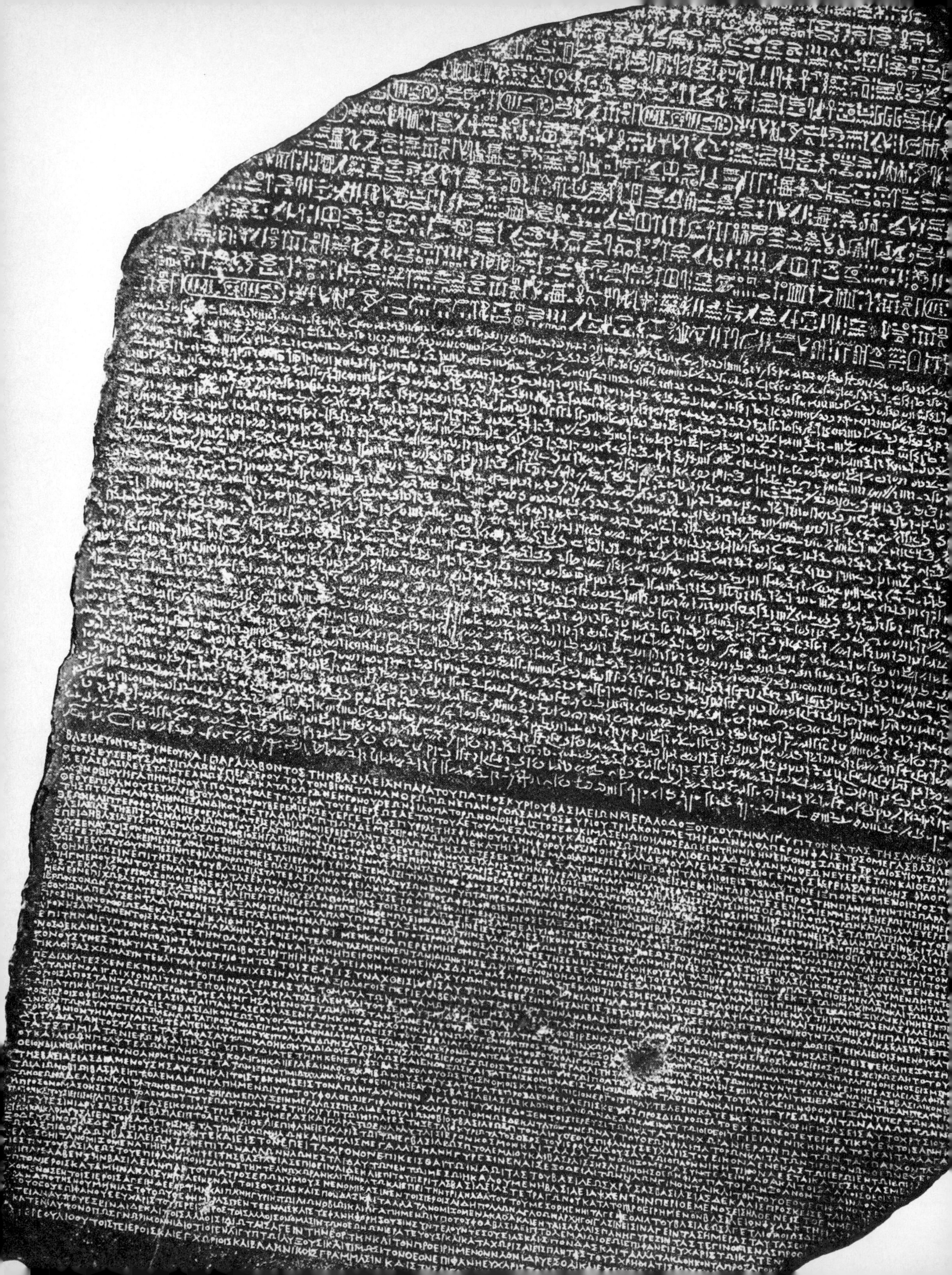

10. The Rosetta Stone

Imagine a message so difficult that it took fourteen years to decode! Think of a scholar working day and night to learn the meanings of ancient writings. Jean Francois Champollion of France worked on a project of this kind for many years. The work was very difficult but he refused to be defeated. The text he studied was carved on a stone found in Rosetta, Egypt. It was named the Rosetta Stone.

The stone was first found by a French engineer. He did not think it was important. So he threw it away. But an archaeologist picked it up. There were strange carvings on the stone called hieroglyphics. These are characters in Egyptian picture writing. Birds with tall crowns, snakes, and peculiar figures were carved on the stone.

The text was written in three languages. Greek, hieroglyphics, and ancient Egyptian were on the stone. Champollion translated the Greek section. Then he compared the Greek words with the hieroglyphics. He also knew Coptic. This helped him recognize many Egyptian words. Finally, in 1828, the riddle of the Rosetta Stone was solved. Because of Champollion, today scholars can read hieroglyphics and learn the history of the ancient past.

Make a List

There are eight vocabulary words in this lesson. In the story, they are boxed in color. Copy the vocabulary words here.

1. _____
2. _____
3. _____
4. _____

5. _____
6. _____
7. _____
8. _____

75

Make an Alphabetical List _____

Here are the eight words you copied on the previous page. Write them in alphabetical order in the blank spaces below.

engineer   text   peculiar   decode
scholar   translated defeated   archaeologist

1. _____   5. _____

2. _____   6. _____

3. _____   7. _____

4. _____   8. _____

What Do the Words Mean? _____

Here are some meanings for the eight vocabulary words in this lesson. Four words have been written beside their meanings. Write the other four words next to their meanings.

1. _____ words and sentences; stories

2. *scholar* _____ professor; person of learning

3. _____ conquered; overcame

4. _____ solve a puzzle; find an answer

5. *archaeologist* _____ person who studies ancient life and cultures; scientist

6. *engineer* _____ person who builds roads and bridges; a specialist in technical fields

7. _____ strange; unusual

8. *translated* _____ put into words of a different language; made understandable

Phonics: Suffixes

Suffixes are one or more letters which are attached to the *end* of words. They also have their own meanings and change the meaning of the new word.

There are many suffixes in our language. You will review the most common ones. Study them carefully. Let's look at some common suffixes and their meanings:

Suffix	Meaning	Word with suffix	Meaning
ful	full; full of	hand<u>ful</u>	a hand that is full
less	not any; without	home<u>less</u>	without a home
est	the most	kind<u>est</u>	the most kind
er	a person or thing	teach<u>er</u>	person who teaches
ish	like	child<u>ish</u>	like a child
ly	in what way	quiet<u>ly</u>	done in a quiet way

Here are eight sentences. Read them carefully and add the correct suffix. The suffix should come from the list above. The first one has been done as an example.

1. He ate the pizza slow *ly* _____.

2. That African dancer is grace_____.

3. If you don't study for a test, you're fool_____.

4. Whom do you think is a good speak_____?

5. He's liked because he's cheer_____.

6. She's the kind_____ lady on the block.

7. Astronauts are fear_____.

8. I want to be a garden_____.

Find the Synonyms

A **synonym** is a word that means the same, or nearly the same, as another word. *Happy* and *glad* are synonyms.

The column on the left contains the eight key words in the story. To the right of each key word are three other words or groups of words. Two of these are synonyms for the key word. Circle the two synonyms.

1. peculiar	ordinary	strange	odd
2. engineer	technical director	weapon carrier	bridge designer
3. decode	send a message	translate	solve a puzzle
4. defeated	overcome	seated	conquered
5. text	writings	words and sentences	old papers
6. scholar	professor	wise person	sports announcer
7. archaeologist	one who studies past life	one who teaches children	one who studies ancient people
8. translated	guessed	decoded	interprted

Using Your Language: Check Your Spelling

There are many words in our language that are often misspelled. These words are spelled incorrectly so many times that they are sometimes called *spelling demons*. (Note: a demon is a devil or evil spirit—and these words cause trouble.) We have given you a correct spelling and an incorrect one. Underline the correct spelling. Then write the word on the line provided. The first one has been done as an example.

Correct Spelling

writing	writting	*writing*
athelete	athlete	
government	goverment	
interesting	intresting	
across	accross	
cafateria	cafeteria	
sandwich	sandwitch	

Use Your Own Words

Look at the picture. What words come into your mind other than the ones you matched with their synonyms? Write them on the blank lines below. To help you get started, here are two good words:

1. *language* 5. _____

2. *writing*   6. _____

3. _____ 7. _____

80 4. _____ 8. _____

Complete the Story

Here are the eight vocabulary words for this lesson:

engineer   translated   text   scholar
archaeologist   defeated   decode   peculiar

There are four blank spaces in the story below. Four vocabulary words have already been used in the story. They are underlined. Use the other four words to fill in the blank spaces.

The engineer tripped on a large stone. He didn't pay much attention to it. He had more important things to do, like building roads and bridges. So he threw it away. But an _____ noticed the strange carvings on the stone. These peculiar carvings represented Egyptian picture writing. They were called hieroglyphics. For centuries this strange picture writing confused scientists. They just couldn't figure out what the pictures meant.

But the _____ Jean Francois Champollion was determined to work it out. He would _____ these messages if it took a lifetime. He would not be _____. Actually, it was fourteen years before he translated the writings. He found the key by comparing three different languages. Once he solved the riddle, scientists began to work on another text. They could now learn the history of the past.

11. At The Top Again

It's a long way from New Jersey to Hollywood. But John Travolta made it. He had the usual bit parts along the way. There was the road tour of *Grease*. At first he was only a member of the chorus. Five years later, he starred in the movie version. The reviews were good. The public was becoming aware of his acting skills. When *Saturday Night Fever* appeared, his stardom seemed certain.

Saturday Night Fever was a smash hit. The public responded to Travolta's charm and talent. Disco dancing became a national pastime because of his movie. But after *Saturday Night Fever* and *Grease,* Travolta's career seemed to go into a brief decline. His new movies were not very successful. Some people started to question his ability. Then along came the film *Urban Cowboy*. Once again, people lined up to buy tickets. Travolta's career rebounded. The star had returned.

People respond to fame in different ways. Some cannot take the pressures. Others begin to believe all the press notices. But John Travolta has not neglected his family or the people who helped him. He continues to work hard. He has plans for other films. For millions of fans, the Travolta magic remains as strong as ever.

Make a List

There are eight vocabulary words in this lesson. In the story, they are boxed in color. Copy the vocabulary words here.

1. _____   5. _____

2. _____   6. _____

3. _____   7. _____

4. _____   8. _____

Make an Alphabetical List _____

Here are the eight words you copied on the previous page. Write them in alphabetical order in the blank spaces below.

chorus   rebounded   press   version
pastime   neglected   decline   responded

1. _____   5. _____

2. _____   6. _____

3. _____   7. _____

4. _____   8. _____

What Do the Words Mean? _____

Here are some meanings for the eight vocabulary words in this lesson. Four words have been written beside their meanings. Write the other four words next to their meanings.

1. _____ singing or dancing group; performers

2. *pastime* hobby; pleasant way of spending spare time

3. *neglected* ignored; overlooked

4. _____ bounced back; returned

5. *decline* falling off; downward movement

6. _____ news services; newspapers and magazines

7. *version* a different form; another way of presenting a story

84

8. _____ answered; replied

Phonics: Reviewing Consonants _____

In Lesson 1 you had practice exercises dealing with consonants. Look at the consonants again. In the alphabet, all the letters are consonants except the vowels *a, e, i, o, u,* and sometimes *y.*

A consonant can be at the beginning of a word, or in the middle of a word, or at the end of a word. For example: in the word *rest*

> *r* is a beginning consonant
> *s* is a middle consonant
> *t* is a final consonant

Here are ten words. See how well you can recognize the beginning, middle, and final consonants. After each word, write the letter *B* if the word contains a beginning consonant, the letter *M* for a middle consonant, and the letter *F* for a final consonant.

Each word in the list contains consonants. The first one has been done as an example.

read   *B. F* _____

answer   _____

question   _____

book   _____

creep   _____

umbrella   _____

writing   _____

olympics   _____

use   _____

orange   _____

Find the Synonyms _____

A **synonym** is a word that means the same, or nearly the same, as another word. *Happy* and *glad* are synonyms.

The column on the left contains the eight key words in the story. To the right of each key word are three other words or groups of words. Two of these are synonyms for the key word. Circle the two synonyms.

1. responded	answered	ignored	replied
2. chorus	audience	performers	singing group
3. neglected	watched	overlooked	ignored
4. rebounded	returned	disappeared	bounced back
5. press	newspapers	movies	magazines
6. decline	upward	downward	a falling off
7. pastime	recreation	chore	entertainment
8. version	another form	another way	the original

Using Your Language: Adjectives _____

An **adjective** is a word that describes a person, place, or thing. For example, in the sentence "John Travolta is a handsome and skilled actor," *handsome* and *skilled* are adjectives which describe actor. Underline the adjectives in the following sentences. The first one has been done as an example.

1. We waited in the <u>long</u>, <u>cold</u> line to see our <u>favorite</u> singer.

2. Disco dancing has become a national pastime.

3. Many of John's faithful fans send him long, interesting letters.

4. The cruel, bitter reviews of his movie almost made the actor quit.

5. Behind those good looks is a sensitive, intelligent, and thoughtful actor.

Use Your Own Words

Look at the picture. What words come into your mind other than the ones you matched with their synonyms? Write them on the blank lines below. To help you get started, here are two good words:

1. *lights*   5. _____
2. *dancer*   6. _____
3. _____   7. _____
4. _____   8. _____

Complete the Story _____

Here are the eight vocabulary words for this lesson:

pastime   chorus   rebounded   version
press   neglected   responded   decline

There are four blank spaces in the story below. Four vocabulary words have already been used in the story. They are underlined. Use the other four words to fill in the blank spaces.

If disco dancing is a national <u>pastime</u>, a lot of the credit must go to John Travolta. His dancing in the movie *Saturday Night Fever* received outstanding _____ notices. Critics praised his acting as well as his good looks. He was more than just a handsome _____ boy. He was an actor who would not be <u>neglected</u>. He repeated his success in *Grease*. His future looked bright. Then his career went into a brief _____. His new movies were not well received at the box office. Some people thought he was through. But John had other ideas. He read a <u>version</u> of *Urban Cowboy* in a national magazine. He accepted the starring role in the movie. It became a big smash hit. Travolta's career <u>rebounded</u>. Once again, the public _____ to his talent. His hard work and planning paid off.

12. QUEEN OF THE FAIRWAYS

Nancy Lopez is the hottest golfer to blaze across the fairways in years. In her first two years as a pro, she was twice voted player of the year. As a rookie, she set a record for money earnings. Nancy also won nine tournaments. She managed to win five in a row—another record. She continued her great play in 1979 by winning eight tournaments.

Her fans are called "Nancy's Navy." The name comes from Arnold Palmer's fans, better known as "Arnold's Army." They are thrilled by her success. Even rivals who compete against her, admire her. Nancy is gracious and charming as well as a great golfer.

Her life is an American success story. She was born into a poor Mexican-American family in California. Later her family moved to Roswell, New Mexico. There, her father took up golf. She accompanied him on the golf course from the age of seven. Her father taught her all he knew about golf.

Nancy has many golfing skills. She has an excellent putting game. Her swing has great power. Nancy is aggressive. She likes to win. She is cool in tight spots. That's another indication of the true champion. Nancy Lopez, golf pro, is delighted to be "Queen of the Fairways."

Make a List

There are eight vocabulary words in this lesson. In the story, they are boxed in color. Copy the vocabulary words here.

1. _____   5. _____

2. _____   6. _____

3. _____   7. _____

4. _____   8. _____

91

Make an Alphabetical List _____

Here are the eight words you copied on the previous page. Write them in alphabetical order in the blank spaces below.

rivals   accompanied   delighted   fairways
rookie   indication   gracious   tournaments

1. _____   5. _____

2. _____   6. _____

3. _____   7. _____

4. _____   8. _____

What Do the Words Mean? _____

Here are some meanings for the eight vocabulary words in this lesson. Four words have been written beside their meanings. Write the other four words next to their meanings.

1. _____ opposing players; opponents

2. *accompanied* joined; went with

3. _____ highly pleased; joyous

4. *fairways* golf courses; usually the green areas where the long drives are hit

5. _____ beginner; person who is new at a game

6. *indication* sign; mark

7. *gracious* charming; pleasant in manners and attitude

8. _____ athletic contests; matches, as in tennis or golf

Phonics: Reviewing Short Vowels_____

In Lesson 3 you learned the short vowel sounds and did some practice exercises. In this lesson you will review the short vowel sounds. Here are some examples of each of the short vowel sounds.

short ă	short ĕ	short ĭ	short ŏ	short ŭ
măp	wĕt	fĭt	mŏp	hŭt

The following story is true. Read it and underline the words with short vowel sounds. The first line has been done as an example.

The Circus Elephant

<u>Did</u> you read about <u>Pinky</u>, the <u>circus</u> <u>elephant</u>? He'd turn his head away whenever his master gave him water. He only liked to drink Pepsi Cola. Pinky would put his trunk into the barrel and guzzle up all the Pepsi. He drank so fast that his trunk sucked up a lot of air. Then he'd belch and burp. All the circus people would gather and watch Pinky for their evening fun.

Find the Synonyms _____

A **synonym** is a word that means the same, or nearly the same, as another word. *Happy* and *glad* are synonyms.

The column on the left contains the eight key words in the story. To the right of each key word are three other words or groups of words. Two of these are synonyms for the key word. Circle the two synonyms.

1. rookie	manager	beginner	starter
2. delighted	pleased	joyful	disappointed
3. tournaments	athletic meets	contests	players
4. accompanied	joined	left behind	went along
5. indication	mask	mark	sign
6. rivals	opponents	winners	competitors
7. gracious	athletic	charming	pleasant
8. fairways	golf courses	beautiful weather	green areas

Using Your Language: Antonyms

Antonyms are words that are opposite in meaning. For example, *good* and *bad*, *fast* and *slow* are antonyms. Here are antonyms for six of the vocabulary words. See if you can find the vocabulary words, and write them in the blank spaces on the left. The first one has been done as an example.

Vocabulary Word	**Antonym**
1. *fairways*	sand traps
2. _____	teammates
3. _____	veteran
4. _____	unfriendly
5. _____	separated from
6. _____	disappointed

Use Your Own Words ──────────────

Look at the picture. What words come into your mind other than the ones you matched with their synonyms? Write them on the blank lines below. To help you get started, here are two good words:

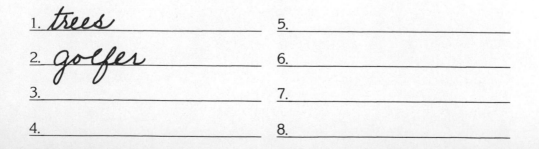

1. *trees*   5. _____
2. *golfer*   6. _____
3. _____   7. _____

4. _____   8. _____

Complete the Story

Here are the eight vocabulary words for this lesson:

rivals   accompanied   delighted   fairways
rookie   indication   gracious   tournaments

There are four blank spaces in the story below. Four vocabulary words have already been used in the story. They are underlined. Use the other four words to fill in the blank spaces.

There are many ways to applaud a great athlete. To compare a golfer to Jack Nicklaus is high praise indeed. It gives the reader some <u>indication</u> of Nancy Lopez's talents. She is a real marvel on the _____. She has all-around skills. She can hit a golf ball as long as most pros. Her putting is great. Most important, she is cool and steady under pressure. As a <u>rookie</u> in 1978, she won nine _____. Her earnings also set a record. Now when Nancy plays, she is _____ by hundreds of admirers. These fans are known as "Nancy's Navy."

Nancy's <u>rivals</u> are the first to admit that she deserves her success. They like her as a person. She is friendly and behaves well on and off the course. When people ask for autographs, she is <u>delighted</u> to give them. She remembers the hard times as well as the good. While she loves to win, she is _____ in defeat. She can smile and say, "Wait until the next tournament."

13. BORN TO SING

There was always music in his home. His family sang for fun. They sang while they worked. They sang for friends and for each other. This was the atmosphere in which Luciano (LU-chee-on-oo) Pavarotti (PAV-uh-rot-ee) grew up.

His father was a baker. But he had the soul of a singer. The family's life focused on music. His father enjoyed singing at community meetings. His dad wanted him to become a singer. His mother was more careful. She hoped he would be an accountant.

Luciano studied music and singing. He never thought of being an opera star. Instead he became a primary school teacher. But when he won an important tenor contest he decided to work on his music. That same year he made his debut in *La Boheme.* Success soon followed. The people loved him. They devoured his music. He had the winning mixture of voice and looks. His handsome masculine appearance won many admirers.

In just two and one-half years, Luciano became a famous figure. Now he is recognized as one of the world's leading tenors.

Make a List

There are eight vocabulary words in this lesson. In the story, they are boxed in color. Copy the vocabulary words here.

1. _____   5. _____

2. _____   6. _____

3. _____   7. _____

4. _____   8. _____

Make an Alphabetical List _____

Here are the eight words you copied on the previous page. Write them in alphabetical order in the blank spaces below.

atmosphere   tenor   masculine   community
accountant   primary   devoured   focused

1. _____   5. _____

2. _____   6. _____

3. _____   7. _____

4. _____   8. _____

What Do the Words Mean? _____

Here are some meanings for the eight vocabulary words in this lesson. Four words have been written beside their meanings. Write the other four words next to their meanings.

1. *tenor* _____ male singer, usually in opera

2. _____ people living together in a particular town or district; group of people

3. _____ manly; full of strength and vigor

4. *focused* _____ concentrated; centered

5. _____ first three years of school; usually refers to grades K-3

6. *atmosphere* environment; mood

7. *accountant* a person who keeps business accounts; skilled at working with numbers

8. _____ took in greedily with ears, eyes, or mind; absorbed completely

Phonics: Reviewing Prefixes

Remember, prefixes are one or more letters attached to the beginning of a root word. Prefixes have different meanings. When they join words they change the meaning of that word. There are many prefixes in our language. Here are a few more to help you figure out word meanings. For example:

> *mis*   means *wrong* or *mistake*
>
> *mis* + *trial* = mistake in a trial
>
> *fore*   means *before* or *in front*
>
> *fore* + *tell* = tell or predict what will happen in the future
>
> *inter*   means *between* or *among*
>
> *inter* + *national* = among the nations

In the following list, connect the prefix with the word. Write the new word and its meaning. The first one has been done as an example.

Prefix		Root Word		New Word
fore	+	man	=	*foreman*
mis	+	start	=	_____
inter	+	state	=	_____
de	+	frost	=	_____
auto	+	biography	=	_____
co	+	operate	=	_____

Find the Synonyms _____

A **synonym** is a word that means the same, or nearly the same, as another word. *Happy* and *glad* are synonyms.

The column on the left contains the eight key words in the story. To the right of each key word are three other words or groups of words. Two of these are synonyms for the key word. Circle the two synonyms.

1. community	group of people	town of people	list of people
2. masculine	weak	manly	strong
3. devoured	absorbed	rejected	took in hungrily
4. primary	early school years	grades 9-12	grades K-3
5. focused	concentrated	centered	wandered
6. atmosphere	mood	environment	habits
7. tenor	singer	designer	opera star
8. accountant	bookkeeper	teacher	examiner

Using Your Language: Nouns

Nouns are words used to show names of persons, places, things, actions, ideas, and qualities. There are two kinds of nouns, *proper* and *common*. Common nouns are names of any persons, places, or things: traveler, city, box. Proper nouns are names of particular persons, places, or things: Helen, New York City, Sears Tower.

Underline the nouns in each of the sentences below. Place one line under each common noun. Place two lines under each proper noun. The first one has been done as an example.

1. Luciano Pavarotti was born in the town of Modena in Italy.

2. His mother wanted him to be an accountant in a large firm.

3. His father dreamed of his appearance on the stage of La Scala.

4. The tour of Australia with the great Joan Sutherland is one of his fondest memories.

5. Any opera lover can recite the great roles sung by Pavarotti.

6. Wouldn't you love to tour the great cities of Spain, Holland, and France?

7. Pavarotti made his debut in Italian opera as Rudolpho in *La Boheme*.

8. The old singer loved to tell tales of his great performance at the Metropolitan Opera House.

Use Your Own Words

Look at the picture. What words come into your mind other than the ones you matched with their synonyms? Write them on the blank lines below. To help you get started, here are two good words:

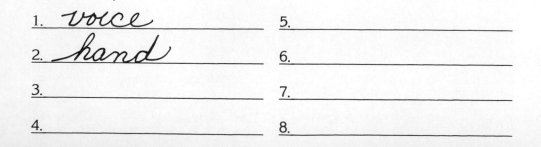

1. *voice*   5. _____

2. *hand*   6. _____

3. _____   7. _____

104   4. _____   8. _____

Complete the Story

Here are the eight vocabulary words for this lesson:

tenor	focused	primary	masculine
atmosphere	community	accountant	devoured

There are four blank spaces in the story below. Four vocabulary words have already been used in the story. They are underlined. Use the other four words to fill in the blank spaces.

In *World of Vocabulary,* Book A, there is a story about Beverly Sills. Another great opera star is the Italian _____, Luciano Pavarotti. Both stars love the atmosphere of opera. Each had problems to overcome before reaching the top. And both are highly respected in the special community of opera lovers.

Luciano's early life _____ on singing. His father was an amateur singer who wanted Luciano to become a professional. His mother was more cautious. She wanted him to become an accountant. Luciano, instead, became a teacher. He taught in a _____ school. But he continued to study music and singing. He finally got his big chance.

His debut in Italian opera was in *La Boheme.* He was an immediate hit. The audience devoured his music. They wanted more. They had discovered a star who had the right combination of voice and _____ good looks. From then on, he was invited to appear at the world's most famous opera houses.

14. Britain's Pride

In 1954, Roger Bannister did the impossible. He ran the mile in under four minutes. Since then, the four-minute mark has been broken many times. One of the record breakers is Sebastian Coe. Coe is a slim, 23-year-old Englishman. He is 5 ft. 9 inches tall and weighs 129 pounds. Many say he is the best middle-distance runner in the world. Between 1979 and 1980, he held world records in four major events. He set marks at 800, 1,000, and 1,500 meters, and also the mile. His feats have brought pride back to Britain.

Coe lives in Sheffield, England. He is a college graduate who plans a career in business or journalism. For the time being, his main interest is running. He is assisted by his father, who is his coach and trainer. Sebastian Coe runs from 50 to 70 miles (80-112 km) a week.

Coe's chief rival is Steve Ovett, another Englishman. They differ in personality. Coe is friendly and talkative. Ovett is reserved and dislikes giving interviews. Both take turns at breaking each other's records. At the 1980 Summer Olympics, Ovett won the 800 meters. Coe won the 1,500-meter race. Fans gaze in awe as these two superb athletes try to outrun each other.

Make a List

There are eight vocabulary words in this lesson. In the story, they are boxed in color. Copy the vocabulary words here.

1. _____

2. _____

3. _____

4. _____

5. _____

6. _____

7. _____

8. _____

107

Make an Alphabetical List _____

Here are the eight words you copied on the previous page. Write them in alphabetical order in the blank spaces below.

| impossible | pride | assisted | reserved |
| slim | journalism | talkative | awe |

1. _____   5. _____

2. _____   6. _____

3. _____   7. _____

4. _____   8. _____

What Do the Words Mean? _____

Here are some meanings for the eight vocabulary words in this lesson. Four words have been written beside their meanings. Write the other four words next to their meanings.

1. *pride* _____ self-respect; having a good feeling about one's self or country

2. _____ quiet manner; keeps to himself/herself

3. *awe* _____ amazement; wonder

4. _____ hopeless; unable to be done

5. *journalism* _____ the business of reporting the news; newspaper work

6. _____ helped; aided

7. *talkative* _____ one who talks a great deal; gabby

8. _____ thin; slender

Phonics: Reviewing Digraphs _____

In Lesson 4 you learned about beginning digraphs. Now you're going to learn about digraphs at the *end* of words.

Let's review. Digraphs are two consonant sounds that make a single sound. For example:

<u>wh</u> as in <u>wh</u>en (beginning digraph)
<u>sh</u> as in wa<u>sh</u> (final digraph)
<u>ch</u> as in dit<u>ch</u> (final digraph)

Here are some more examples of final digraphs:

ch	**sh**	**gh**	**ph**	**th**	**ck**	**gn**
ea<u>ch</u>	bru<u>sh</u>	lau<u>gh</u>	gra<u>ph</u>	wi<u>th</u>	ba<u>ck</u>	si<u>gn</u>

Underline the words in the story below that contain consonant digraphs. The digraphs can be in any part of the word. The first sentence has been done as an example.

The Pitcher

<u>Sh</u>ep <u>Wh</u>itney, the pit<u>ch</u>er, looked <u>Th</u>urmond, the coa<u>ch</u>, strai<u>gh</u>t in the eye. "I'm not a bench warmer. I'm going out there to beat them. Just watch me pitch. I won't give up!"

The coach shouted and crushed his hat. "This is the World Series, Shep! You're pitching as if you were all thumbs. You belong in the bush leagues. And you call yourself a champ!

Find the Synonyms _____

A **synonym** is a word that means the same, or nearly the same, as another word. *Happy* and *glad* are synonyms.

The column on the left contains the eight key words in the story. To the right of each key word are three other words or groups of words. Two of these are synonyms for the key word. Circle the two synonyms.

1. pride	wrongdoing	good-feeling	self-respect
2. awe	wonder	amazement	sadness
3. reserved	faithful	quiet	not talkative
4. impossible	can't be done	completed	hopeless
5. journalism	selling newspapers	newspaper work	reporting news
6. assisted	aided	stopped	helped
7. talkative	chatty	gossipy	moody
8. slim	thin	slender	softly

Using Your Language: Contractions ———

Many times two words are shortened into one by leaving out one or more letters, and putting in an apostrophe. The shortened word is called a contraction. For example, *I'll* is the contraction for *I will*. *Don't* is the contraction for *do not*.

In the left hand column are some common contractions. Write the two words the contraction stands for in the right hand column. The first one has been done as an example.

Contraction	Two Words Contraction Stands For
we'll	*we will*
he'll	_____
wouldn't	_____
hadn't	_____
we're	_____
I'm	_____

Use Your Own Words

Look at the picture. What words come into your mind other than the ones you matched with their synonyms? Write them on the blank lines below. To help you get started, here are two good words:

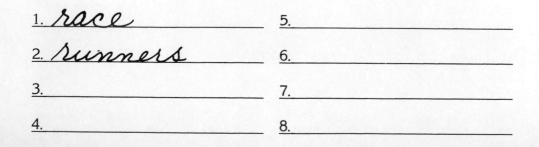

1. *race*   5. _____

2. *runners*   6. _____

3. _____   7. _____

4. _____   8. _____

Complete the Story

Here are the eight vocabulary words for this lesson:

impossible	pride	talkative	reserved
slim	journalism	assisted	awe

There are four blank spaces in the story below. Four vocabulary words have already been used in the story. They are underlined. Use the other four words to fill in the blank spaces.

The rivalry between Coe and Ovett is an intense one. They take great pleasure in breaking each other's records. Fans watch in <u>awe</u> to see who will run faster. Both athletes take great _____ in their skills. Both also differ in personality. Coe is friendly and <u>talkative</u>. Ovett, on the other hand, is _____. He dislikes giving interviews. Coe may be more friendly with reporters because he is very interested in _____. Their training methods also differ. The <u>slim</u>, athletic Coe runs 50-70 miles (31-43 km) a week. He is _____ by his father, who is his coach and trainer. Ovett will run 160 miles (257 km) a week to keep in shape. One tries for speed, the other endurance. It will be interesting to see who will win the most races. No record seems <u>impossible</u> as they race against each other.

15. San Gennaro

New York would not be the same without the Festival of San Gennaro. Once a year along Mulberry Street in New York City there is a feast. It is a ten-block spectacle. People come to eat, drink, sing, and dance. Everyone is friendly. There are hundreds of booths in the streets. They overflow with all kinds of Italian food.

For at least a generation people have honored San Gennaro. He was a third-century bishop. It is said that his prayers saved Naples by stopping a huge volcanic eruption.

During the feast, the saint's bust is draped in red ribbons. It is carried through the streets of Little Italy. A service is held in honor of the saint. Then the statue is taken to a shrine where it has the place of honor.

The feast lasts eleven days. Every night is dazzling. There are many arches aglow with the light of two million bulbs. Musicians play love songs. The air is filled with romance. After watching street dances, people eat and make merry until they are weary. Everyone is welcome at the San Gennaro Festival. Perhaps you can join the fun someday.

Make a List

There are eight vocabulary words in this lesson. In the story, they are boxed in color. Copy the vocabulary words here.

1. _____   5. _____

2. _____   6. _____

3. _____   7. _____

4. _____   8. _____

115

Make an Alphabetical List _____

Here are the eight words you copied on the previous page. Write them in alphabetical order in the blank spaces below.

romance   spectacle   weary   dazzling
overflow   bust   eruption   generation

1._____   5._____

2._____   6._____

3._____   7._____

4._____   8._____

What Do the Words Mean? _____

Here are some meanings for the eight vocabulary words in this lesson. Four words have been written beside their meanings. Write the other four words next to their meanings.

1._____   bursting forth of a volcano; throwing out of lava

2._____   tired; worn out

3.*dazzling*_____   shining brightly; glaringly bright

4.*generation*_____   period of time (approximately 30 years); people living during same period of time

5.*spectacle*_____   unusual sight; elaborate show or display

6._____   to flow or spread over; running over the top

7.*bust*_____   piece of sculpture representing the upper part of the body; a statue

8._____   feeling of love and adventure; affection

116

Phonics: Reviewing Blends _____

In Lesson 6 you were introduced to consonant blends. Remember, blends are made by two or three consonants coming together. They can appear at the beginning, middle, and end of words. In Lesson 6 you worked with beginning blends. Now you will work with blends at the end of words. For example:

st	**sk**	**ng**	**nd**	**nk**	**lf**
feast	desk	bang	sand	thank	self
wrist	flask	rang	end	bank	shelf

Complete the following sentences by supplying a word that ends with a consonant blend. Use only those words that appear in the examples above. The first one has been done as an example.

1. Can you think of a synonym for "loud noise"? The answer is *bang* _____.

2. For the many favors you have done, I say "_____ _____ you."

3. It is a part of your arm above your fingers. It is called your _____.

4. The reference books can be found on the top _____.

5. We had so many good things to eat that our meal could be called a _____.

6. Don't keep too much cash on hand. Deposit it in a _____.

7. If I don't straighten the top of my _____, I'll never find my homework.

8. I can't wait until I reach the _____ of my book so I can find out whom Phyllis marries.

Find the Synonyms

A **synonym** is a word that means the same, or nearly the same, as another word. *Happy* and *glad* are synonyms.

The column on the left contains the eight key words in the story. To the right of each key word are three other words or groups of words. Two of these are synonyms for the key word. Circle the two synonyms.

1. spectacle	spy	display	great show
2. romance	love	affection	foolishness
3. overflow	run over	spread over	move over
4. eruption	throw out	slow down	burst forth
5. dazzling	overpowering with light	puzzling	very bright
6. generation	forgotten time	period of time	people of a time
7. weary	fatigued	overjoyed	tired
8. bust	sculpture of the upper part of the body	statue	shelf

Using Your Language: Capital Letters _____

In each of the following sentences there are words which require capital letters. Rewrite each sentence so the words are correctly capitalized. Remember that capital letters are used in the following places: first word in a sentence; names of people, cars, cities, states, countries, holidays, days of the week, and months of the year. The first one has been done as an example.

1. naples was saved by saint gennaro who stopped the eruption of mt. vesuvious.

   Naples was saved by Saint Gennaro who stopped the eruption of Mt. Vesuvious.

2. every september along mulberry street in new york city there is a festival that honors san gennaro.

   _____

   _____

   _____

3. if you enjoy italian food from rome and genoa, hurry to the booth at the corner of mulberry street and second avenue.

   _____

   _____

   _____

Use Your Own Words ─────────────────

Look at the picture. What words come into your mind other than the ones you matched with their synonyms? Write them on the blank lines below. To help you get started, here are two good words:

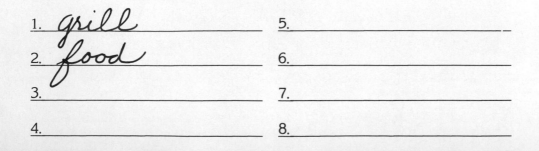

1. *grill* _____   5. _____

2. *food* _____   6. _____

3. _____   7. _____

120   4. _____   8. _____

Complete the Story

Here are the eight vocabulary words for this lesson:

overflow   bust   weary   romance
eruption   generation   dazzling   spectacle

There are four blank spaces in the story below. Four vocabulary words have already been used in the story. They are underlined. Use the other four words to fill in the blank spaces.

You are on your way to the San Gennaro Festival. All year you have waited for this _____ spectacle. Ahead of you is an evening of fun and food. You haven't eaten all day. You know the booths will _____ with all kinds of food. Here's your chance to sample dozens of tasty items. Just don't overdo it.

The colorful parade begins. Hundreds of people crowd around the bust of Saint Gennaro. They rush to pin dollar bills on the red ribbons. Not many people know that Saint Gennaro saved Naples by stopping the _____ of a great volcano.

Late that night you return home. You are _____ from hours of dancing and singing. But everything was so gay and lovely. It was a night of romance. You are pleased that this festival is part of your generation. You hope that it will continue for many more years.

Mini-Dictionary

accompanied *[uh-KUM-puh-need]* joined; went with

accountant *[uh-KOUN-tunt]* a person who keeps business accounts; skilled at working with numbers

accurate *[AK-yur-it]* correct; careful and exact

acrobat *[AK-ruh-bat]* skilled gymnast; expert in tumbling

admitted *[ad-MIT-ted]* given permission to enroll as a student; allowed to enter

aerialist *[AIR-ee-uh-list]* a person who performs on a trapeze; a flyer

agile *[AJ-ul]* having quick, easy movements; limber

alternately *[AWL-tur-nayt-lee]* taking turns; first one, then the other

alert *[uh-LURT]* quick in thought and action; watchful

archaeologist *[ar-Kee-OL-uh-jist]* person who studies ancient life and cultures; scientist

arouses *[uh-ROUZ-es]* stirs up strong feelings; awakens

assisted *[uh-SIST-ed]* helped; aided

atmosphere *[AT-mus-feer]* environment; mood

attractive *[uh-TRAK-tiv]* pretty; pleasing; charming

avenged *[uh-VENJD]* took revenge; got even

average *[AV-er-ij]* a mathematical term used to show how well a batter is doing

awe *[AW]* amazement; wonder

background *[BAK-ground]* past experience; events leading up to the present

bouquets *[boo-KAYS]* bunches of flowers fastened together

bust *[BUST]* piece of sculpture representing the upper part of the body; a statue

candidate *[KAN-dih-date]* person who has been named or proposed for an award or position

chorus *[KAWR-us]* singing or dancing group; performers

collapsed *[kuh-LAPSD]* broke down suddenly; fell down

combines *[kum-BINES]* joins together; mixes

community *[kuh-MYOO-nih-tee]* people living together in a particular town or district; group of people

concert *[KON-surt]* musical performance

construction *[kun-STRUK-shun]* the process of building

dazzling *[DAZ-zling]* shining brightly; glaringly bright

debating *[dih-BAYT-ing]* discussing opposing reasons; arguing

decline *[dih-KLYN]* falling off; downward movement

decode *[dee-KOHD]* solve a puzzle; find an answer

deeds *[DEEDS]* acts; things done

defeated *[dih-FEET-ed]* conquered; overcame

delighted *[dih-LYT-ed]* highly pleased; joyous

demand *[dih-MAND]* ask for; request

designed *[dee-ZIND]* planned; developed

detect *[dih-TEKT]* to discover; to find out

devoured *[dih-VOURD]* took in greedily with ears, eyes, or mind; absorbed completely

ditch *[DITCH]* emergency landing; to land on water

durable *[DYOOR-uh-bul]* long-lasting; difficult to wear out

ease *[EEZ]* natural way or manner

engineer *[en-juh-NEER]* person who builds roads and bridges; a specialist in technical fields

eruption *[ih-RUP-shun]* bursting forth of a volcano; throwing out of lava

exceptional *[ik-SEP-shuh-nul]* way above the average; excellent

fairways *[FAIR-ways]* golf courses; usually the green areas where the long drives are hit

focused *[FO-kusd]* concentrated; centered

foreman *[FOR-man]* person in charge of a group of workers; a boss

fraction *[FRAK-shun]* small part; less than a second in time

generation *[jen-uh-RAY-shun]* period of time (approximately 30 years); people living during same period of time

gracious *[GRAY-shus]* charming; pleasant in manners and attitude

hailed *[HAYLD]* named with pride; called; acclaimed

headlines *[HED-lines]* lines in large type at the top of a newspaper or article

historic *[his-TOR-ik]* famous in history; very important

imported *[im-PORT-ed]* brought into a country

impossible *[im-POS-uh-bul]* hopeless; unable to be done

incredible *[in-KRED-uh-bul]* almost impossible to believe; highly unusual

indication *[in-duh-KAY-shun]* sign; mark

122

intense [in-TENSE] very strong; severe

international [in-tur-NASH-uh-nul] involving two or more nations

journalism [JUR-nuh-liz-um] the business of reporting the news; newspaper work

latter [LAYT-ur] the last of two things mentioned

limited [LIM-ih-tid] kept within certain boundaries; restricted

limits [LIM-its] boundary lines; a person can't go beyond these points

majored [MAY-jurd] concentrated on a major field of study; specialized

masculine [MAS-kyu-lin] manly; full of strength and vigor

mixture [MIKS-chur] combination; something made up by mixing two or more things

mobbed [MOBBD] surrounded by; crowded about

muscle [MUS-ul] tissue made of cells or fibers

natural [NACH-ur-ul] qualities or skills that a person is born with

neglected [nih-GLEKT-ed] ignored; overlooked

pastime [PAS-tym] hobby; pleasant way of spending spare time

peculiar [pih-KYOOL-yur] strange; unusual

photograph [FOH-tuh-graf] picture taken by a camera

plentiful [PLEN-tih-ful] more than enough; abundant

press [PRES] news services; newspapers and magazines

prestige [PRES-tij] influence; excellent reputation

pride [PRYD] self-respect; having a good feeling about one's self or country

primary [PRI-mer-ee] first three years of school; usually refers to grades K-3

professor [pruh-FES-ur] a teacher, usually in a college or university; a learned person

rebel [REB-ul] person who goes against the system; one who resists authority

rebounded [rih-BOUND-ed] bounced back; returned

rejected [rih-JEKT-ed] refused or turned away

research [rih-SURCH] careful study of some field of knowledge; investigation

reserved [rih-ZURVD] quiet manner; keeps to himself

resolved [rih-ZOLVD] determined; fixed in purpose

responded [rih-SPOND-ed] answered; replied

rivals [RY-vuls] opposing players; opponents

romance [roh-MANS] feeling of love and adventure; affection

rookie [ROOK-ee] beginner; person who is new at a game

rotation [roh-TAY-shun] taking turns in a regular order; one following the other

routines [roo-TEENS] series of dance steps or movements

scenery [SEE-nuh-ree] painted scenes or hangings for a stage

scholar [SKOL-ur] professor; person of learning

scientific [sy-en-TIF-ik] done with much thought or knowledge; systematic and exact

skill [SKILL] ability to use one's knowledge in doing something

slim [SLIM] thin; slender

solo [SO-loh] to perform alone; to do by one's self

somersaults [SUM-ur-sawlts] acrobatic stunts; full body turns, forward or backward

spectacle [SPEK-tuh-kul] unusual sight; elaborate show or display

struggle [STRUG-ul] hard battle; a fight

stunt [STUNT] daring trick; display of skill

substances [SUB-stan-ses] materials from which something is made

succeed [suk-SEED] to reach a desired goal

talkative [TAW-kuh-tiv] one who talks a great deal; gabby

tender [TEN-der] gentle; sensitive

tenor [TEN-ur] male singer, usually in opera

text [TEKST] words and sentences; stories

total [TOHT-ul] sum; entire amount

tournaments [TOOR-nuh-munts] athletic contests; matches, as in tennis or golf

translated [trans-LAYT-ed] put into words of a different language; to make understandable

trapeze [tra-PEEZ] short horizontal bar, hung by two ropes, on which aerialists perform

trophy [TROH-fee] a prize, usually a silver cup

tuck [TUK] to pull in; draw in closely

undergo [un-der-GO] to go through; to endure; to experience

uneventful [un-ee-VENT-ful] not exciting; ordinary

version [VUR-shun] a different form; another way of presenting a story

vocalist [VOH-kuh-list] one who sings; singer

weary [WEER-ee] tired; worn out

widows [WID-ohs] women whose husbands have died